Sports Stars

WALTER PAYTON

The Running Machine

By Dick Conrad

CHILDRENS PRESS ®

CHICAGO

Cover photograph: United Press International
Inside photographs courtesy of the following: Bill Smith Photography, pages 8, 10, 16, 18, 21, 22, 24, 26, 30, 31, 34, 35, 39, 40, and 43; Richard Pilling, 36; United Press International, 6, 13, and 33.

Cover photograph: Carl Sissac
Inside photographs courtesy of the following:
Bill Smith Photography, pages 8, 10, 16, 18, 21, 22, 24, 26, 30, 31, 34, 35, 39, 40, and 43
Richard Pilling, page 36
United Press International, pages 6, 13, and 33

Library of Congress Cataloging in Publication Data

Conrad, Dick.
   Walter Payton, the running machine.

   (Sport stars)
   Summary: Highlights the career of running back Walter Payton who started playing professional ball in 1975 with the Chicago Bears.
   1. Payton, Walter, 1954-   —Juvenile literature.
2. Football players—United States—Biography.
[1. Payton, Walter, 1954-   . 2. Football players.
3. Afro-Americans—Biography.]
I. Title. II. Series.
GV939.P39C66   796.33'2'0924 [B] [92]   78-11379
ISBN 0-516-04306-4

1986 Edition

9 10 11 12 R 90 89 88 87 86

Sports Stars

WALTER PAYTON

The Running Machine

All pro football running backs have a goal. They want to gain 1,000 yards in one season. Chicago Bear Walter Payton first did it in 1976. He gave gold watches to his offensive linemen. The watches were engraved:

THANKS FOR THE 1000

WALTER

"Football is a team game," Walter said. "If I were Muhammad Ali in the ring all alone, I could take all the credit. But I'm running out of the backfield. I'm only as good as my ofensive line lets me be."

The Bears like Payton's team spirit. "One of the great things about Walter is that no one can ever get jealous of him. He is a perfect team player," says Bob Avellini. Avellini was a Bear quarterback.

Payton is the most exciting running back in football in recent times. His runs are thrilling. They can silence a crowd. The instant he gets the ball, the stands are quiet. The fans hold their breaths. They know that anything can happen when Walter carries the ball.

Sometimes Walter gets the ball, but he does not carry it—he passes it. He has even taken a turn as a quarterback and did okay.

Walter Payton (left) and Gale Sayers (right). Sayers was a hard act for Payton to follow.

Pro football fans love to watch great running backs in action. Ten years before Payton came, Gale Sayers played for the Bears. He was a great halfback. He was the best running back Chicago fans had ever seen.

Sayers could go through small holes in defensive lines. He raced down the field. He moved fast. He confused tacklers on other teams.

Then Gale Sayers hurt his knee. He had to stop playing football. But the Chicago fans would never forget him.

Walter Payton joined the Bears in 1975. The experts said he was the best college halfback in the country. "Fine," said the Bear fans. "But is he as good as Sayers?" Even before he had a jersey number, Payton was expected to play as well as Sayers. And Sayers was a legend in Chicago.

Walter's first year with the Bears was a disappointment. "I was hoping I could do more as a rookie," he said. "I know Gale Sayers played in this town, and that he was the best there ever was. I used to watch him back home on TV. But we're two different people. Sayers had his style of running. I have mine."

Payton runs with great strength. He uses his strong arms to ward off tacklers. He is only 5 feet, 10 inches tall. But he weighs 210 pounds. Most of this weight is hard muscle. One Bear coach said of Walter: "I just saw him in the locker room, and I thought God must have taken a chisel and said, 'I'm gonna make me a halfback.' "

Besides strength, Walter has great speed and a limber body. He probably could have been an Olympic gymnast. Walter can walk on his hands halfway down a football field. Once he leap-frogged over Bear assistant coach Brad Ecklund. Ecklund is 6 feet, 4 inches tall.

In 1976, the Chicago Bears had a young team. Many were rookies. The Bears were trying hard to win as many games as they lost. The only thing they had to be proud of was Walter Payton. He was leading the league in rushing.

"I want that rushing title. But I want it for my teammates as well as for myself," Walter said. "No one has ever led the league in rushing without a good offensive line in front of him."

Payton still led the league in December. But O.J. Simpson was starting to catch up. Simpson was the star running back of the Buffalo Bills. So Walter tried harder. He always tried to squeeze out an extra yard. Perhaps he tried too hard.

"There was a lot of pressure on Walter, but he made it more intense," said his teammate and friend Mike Adamle. "He felt he was carrying the whole team, that he had to have a great run every time he got the ball."

This need to do well led to Payton's saddest day as a football player.

On the last day of the season the Bears played Denver. Buffalo, with O.J. Simpson, was playing the Baltimore Colts. O.J. trailed Walter by only 9

Buffalo Bill star O.J. Simpson (left) and Bear star Walter Payton (right) talk together bef a game. O.J. and Walter competed for the rushing title in 1976. O.J. won the title by m than 100 yards.

yards. People were interested in this battle for the rushing title. Both games were on TV.

"We had no idea what a great defensive team Denver had," said one Bear lineman later. They were so good that they went to the Super Bowl the next year.

The first points went to the Bears. They scored two touchdowns. Payton had a 21-yard run. But after those touchdowns, the great Denver defense started playing hard. Bronco players swarmed over Payton when he tried end sweeps. Denver linemen held their ground against Bear blockers. They stopped Payton's plunges. Whenever Walter got the ball he was stopped by the Bronco defense.

After a tackle in the third quarter, Payton hurt his ankle. He had to be helped off the field. He sat on the bench next to Noah Jackson. Suddenly, Payton put his face in his hands and cried. He was not in great pain from his ankle. The pain he felt was not from his body. Walter Payton wants to be perfect. On this wintry afternoon in Chicago, he knew he had failed. While a huge TV audience watched, this great player sat on the bench and cried.

The Bears lost to Denver 28 to 14. On the East Coast, O.J. Simpson ran wild. He won the rushing title by more than 100 yards.

"It was, I guess, the low point in my life," Walter told a writer later. "So much had been made of the fact that I had a chance to beat O.J. Simpson out for the rushing title. When I found myself lying there on the field and knew I had failed, I didn't want to get back up."

In time, Walter would forget that sad afternoon. He is a religious man. He believes that whatever happens in his life is the will of God. He also is very close to his mother and his wife. "My wedding day was the most truly satisfying day of my life," he once said.

Payton went home to Columbia, Mississippi. He went home to relax. But he is too active to really relax. On and off the field Walter is in constant motion. He even stands up to play chess. When he is driving, he hates red lights. Walter has

Walter Payton plays for the Chicago Bears. His brother Eddie plays for the Detroit Lions. On Thanksgiving Day, 1977, the Bears played the Lions at Detroit. On that day, Mrs. Payton (shown here with Eddie) saw both sons play football in the same game.

Mrs. Payton, Eddie (behind Walter), Walter, and Walter's wife Connie at the Bear-Lion game on Thanksgiving Day, 1977.

a CB radio. He uses it all the time. His CB nick-name is the "Mississippi Maniac."

Luckily, he has a good hobby for a person with a lot of energy. Walter plays the drums. His drum playing almost kept him from playing football.

The first time Walter stood on his high school football field he was not playing football. He was playing drums for the school band. His brother Eddie was the star halfback for the school team then. "My mom didn't want us both playing," Walter said. "So I played in the band. After Eddie graduated I decided I'd try out for the team."

In his first high school game Walter ran 60 yards for a touchdown.

After high school, Walter went to Jackson State College. There he joined his brother on the team.

Brothers Eddie Payton (left) and Walter Payton (right).

Eddie Payton now plays for the Detroit Lions in the NFL.

Walter was graduated from college in 1975. That fall he started as a halfback with the Chicago Bears.

In 1977 many fans thought the young Chicago Bears could win their division. Then they could enter the playoffs that led to the Super Bowl. But by mid-season the Bears had won only 3 games. They had lost 4. Again the only thing the team had to cheer about was Walter Payton's running.

In October, the Bears played Green Bay. Fullback Roland Harper was hurt in the game. He could not play. Harper is Walter's best friend on the team. "Don't let it get you down," Walter told

Bear fullback Roland Harper (left) and running back Walter Payton (right) are good frier

his friend. "I'll get you 100 yards. A hundred for you and 100 for me." He did. Walter ran for 205 yards that day. He tied an all-time Bear record held by Gale Sayers.

In late November the Bears faced the Minnesota Vikings. They were one of the Bears' toughest foes. On the very first play, Walter took a handoff. He ran 29 yards. No one watching the game knew that this play was the start of the Great Walter Payton Show.

For the rest of that half in Soldier Field, Chicago, Payton ran for long gains. He swept around ends and into the open field. The Vikings were champions of the Central Division. But they were being torn to pieces by the running back wearing number 34. By the end of the first half he had gained 144 yards.

"The record for yards gained in one game is 273." one fan said. "O.J. Simpson set that mark last year. The way Payton is running he could beat it today. I wonder if anyone has told Payton about the record?"

No one had. His teammates know that Walter does not like to talk during a game. He says it breaks his concentration.

The second half started. Walter shook loose from two Viking defenders. He went over the line. He gained 19 yards. Act Two of the Great Walter Payton Show had begun.

There were less than five minutes left to play. Walter swept behind a block by Revie Sorey. He straight-armed one defender. He darted down the sidelines. Then, 58 yards later, he was pushed out of bounds. He now needed only 5 yards to tie the record. Finally, he got the needed yards. Walter Payton's name went into the record book. He had gained 275 yards in one game.

In the locker room, Walter thanked his team for helping him set a new record. He did allow a little self-pride, however.

"Say, Walter," he was asked. "How would you defense Walter Payton?"

"Well," he answered. "The night before the game I'd kidnap Walter Payton."

During this 1977 game with the Minnesota Vikings Walter Payton gained 275 yards. It was a rushing record for number of yards gained in one game.

Walter setting the NFL rushing record in the Viking game.

Payton's effort against the Vikings started the Bears on a winning streak. Chicago played with new confidence. They won game after game. They headed toward the playoffs.

Something happened during this Chicago winning streak. Payton led his team to victories. And the fans finally stopped comparing him to Gale Sayers. They began to value Walter Payton for himself. At last the shadow of Gale Sayers was gone.

"I'm not even thinking about a record," Walter said before the last game of the regular season. "We've got to beat the New York Giants to make the playoffs. That's what I'm going to be thinking of. Victory, not a record."

Because of Walter's rushing record in the Viking game, the NFL asked the Bears for Walter's jersey and the football used in the game. They are now hanging in the Football Hall of Fame.

Thick ice coated the field at the Bear-Giant game in 1977. This ice would keep Walter Payton from beating O.J. Simpson's rushing record of 2,003 yards in a single season. But if the Bears could win the game they would meet the Dallas Cowboys in the playoffs.

Walter was talking about a record set in 1973. He was still a junior in college. That year, O.J. Simpson rushed for 2,003 yards. It was the highest single season total ever. Payton needed 195 yards to tie that record.

He went to the stadium that day. He knew he had no chance for the record. An ice storm had hit New York. The field was thick with ice. It would have been great for a hockey game.

For four quarters the teams slipped and slid. The game ended with a 9 to 9 tie score. They would have to play one quarter of sudden death. The first team to score would win. If neither team scored the game would stay tied. That would keep the Bears from being in the playoffs. They had to win this game.

Thousands of fans watched on TV. The over-time period began. The fans held their breaths.

Twice the Bears moved close enough to try a field goal. Twice they missed their chance. Less than one minute was left on the clock. Avellini threw a short pass to Payton. Walter turned. He found a New York defender right in front of him. Payton pushed the man out of his way. He advanced the ball 14 yards. It was on the Giant 11-yard line. No time outs were left.

The Bear field-goal unit raced onto the field. The ball was snapped, set down, and kicked. A wild cheer roared out from almost every home in town. On the field, huge Bear players danced with each other. They had won! The Chicago Bears were going to the playoffs.

Walter watching his teammates in action.

The Bears were in the 1977 playoffs (above) but they couldn't beat the strong Dallas Cowboys.

The Bears' joy was short-lived. One week later they lost to the Dallas Cowboys.

After the game, coach Tom Landry of Dallas spoke. He said, "You can't appreciate Walter Payton unless you are on the sidelines watching him. He's so strong. We were hitting him with two and three men. He's one of the great ones."

Walter's next game was the Pro Bowl in January, 1978. At that game he was given a trophy. He had been voted the Most Valuable Player of the 1977 season. He had had one of the greatest years of any running back in NFL history. The 1,853 yards he gained gave him the rushing title for 1977. He also scored 16 touchdowns and 96 points. That was high for the league.

In 1984 Walter exceeded Jim Brown's record of 13,309 yards gained rushing. In 1986 he passed the 15,000 mark.

Finally in 1986, the Chicago Bears went to the Super Bowl. Although Payton didn't score a touchdown, the Bears beat the New England Patriots 46 to 10.

Walter finally was with a winning team and he had a Super Bowl ring. He is still the greatest running back in the history of pro football.

CHRONOLOGY

1954 —Walter Payton is born in Columbia, Mississippi on July 25.

1961 —At the age of seven Walter starts playing the drums. Drumming will remain his favorite hobby.

1965 —Gale Sayers joins the Chicago Bears and becomes a local hero. Ten years later Chicago fans would expect Walter to become as good a running back as Sayers.

1967 —Walter starts Columbia High School, but he does not join the football team. Instead he is a drummer in the school band.

1969 —During his junior year Walter decides to play high school football. In his first game he runs 60 yards for a touchdown.

1971 —Walter enters Jackson State College.

1973 —While Walter is a junior in college, O.J. Simpson rushes for a record 2,003 yards with the Buffalo Bills. Payton would challenge that record four years later.

1974 —At the conclusion of his college career Walter has totaled 464 points scored to set a college record.

1975
Feb. —Walter graduates from Jackson State College.

Sept. —Payton starts as halfback for the Chicago Bears.

1976
Nov. —Walter leads the NFL in running. It appears he will win the rushing title.

Dec. —On his most disappointing day as a football player Payton is unable to move the ball against the strong Denver Bronco defense and loses the rushing title to O.J. Simpson.

1977
Nov. —Walter runs for 275 yards in a game against Minnesota. This breaks the single-game rushing record established the year before by O.J. Simpson.

Dec. —In overtime the Bears beat the New York Giants 12-9 to enter the playoff. Payton finishes the year with 1,852 yards gained, 16 touchdowns, and 96 points. All these are league-leading totals.

1978 —At the Pro Bowl Walter accepts the Most Valuable Player award. He also scores the winning touchdown and is elected MVP of the Pro Bowl even though he claims his playing was "mediocre."

1983 —Walter becomes the fourth NFL rusher to gain 11,000 yards.

1984 —Walter exceeds Jim Brown's record by 997 yards, with a total of 13,309 yards gained rushing.

1985-86—Walter scores 11 touchdowns and rushes for 1,551 yards as the Bears win Super Bowl XX.

1985   —Walter scores 11 touchdowns and rushes for 1,551 yards as the Bears win
         Super Bowl XX.

1986   —Early in the season, Walter surpasses 15,000 yards gained rushing and
         scores his 100th touchdown.

ABOUT THE AUTHOR

In his youth Mr. Conrad was a mediocre basketball player, a poor baseball player, and an absolute disaster as a football player. Consequently, he spent many hours on the sidelines of athletic fields watching more gifted athletes perform. From an early age he became a fan.

Mr. Conrad was especially pleased when Childrens Press asked him to write this book on Walter Payton. Mr. Conrad was born and grew up in a Chicago neighborhood that was just a few blocks from Wrigley Field, where the Chicago Bears used to play ball. Mr. Conrad is a lifelong Chicago Bear fan, and thinks that Walter Payton is the greatest running back in history.